Costuming Classic Drama Queens

By David Wolfe

During Hollywood's Golden Age of the 1930s and 1940s, cinematic storytelling reached the pinnacle of artistry, seen by as many as 80 million Americans every week. The studio system was a dream factory that produced musicals, comedies, Westerns, mysteries and dramatic stories starring Classic Drama Queens. Literally larger than life, their photogenic faces were projected in close-ups as they suffered, sighed, raged, wept, blushed, glowed and sometimes died, while seldom messing their carefully coiffed hair or Max Factor perfection. Their potent appeal included the ability to wear clothes with panache, creations by talented costume designers including Adrian, Orry-Kelly, and Edith Head. Costumes were the key to magical movie moments such as Bette Davis in *Now, Voyager* walking down the ship's gangplank, transformed from frump to sophisticate. (Top right.) A gown could upstage a star, as when Joan Crawford, in *Letty Lynton*, stood in the moonlight wearing a cloud of white organdy ruffles. (Right.) Macy's Cinema Shop claimed to have sold 500,000 copies (surely an exaggeration).

Paper dolls of film stars were an important part of the promotional machine that included movie magazines, fashion photographs and product endorsements. Six stand-out stars qualify as Classic Drama Queens. They are the subjects of this book, paper dolls with costumes from some of the best dramas ever seen on the screen.

Greta Garbo has been called the greatest motion picture actress of all time as well as the most beautiful woman in the world. So famous that her first name became superfluous, Garbo was born in Sweden in 1905, modeled and studied acting. She came to Hollywood and reigned supreme for more than a decade. A silent film star, she transitioned smoothly into sound films with 1930's *Anna Christie*. "Garbo talks!" was big news. Her body was athletic and her posture slouched, yet Adrian's designs transformed Garbo into a goddess, whether in the languid lines of contemporary '20s and '30s styles or period costumes smothered in ruffles, spangles and bows. Her arched brows and simple coiffures influenced a generation and the side-tilted Empress Eugenie hat she wore started a decade-long millinery trend. In stunning costumes, she played exotic spy *Mata Hari* (1931), then Sweden's *Queen Christina* (1933) and *Anna Karenina* (1935). Tragic *Camille* (1936) is considered her finest performance. *Ninotchka* (1939), a comedy, was publicized with the tag line, "Garbo laughs!"

Continued on inside back cover.

B-1…Bette Davis in *Now, Voyager* (1942). Designer: Orry-Kelly.
J-2…Joan Crawford in *Letty Lynton* (1932). Designer: Adrian.

Deluxe Tailoring… Smart suits, coats and gowns established the taste and furs attested to the affluence of the sophisticated leading ladies. A carefully chosen hat, handbag and gloves were the finishing touches. I-1…Joan Crawford in *Mildred Pierce* (1945). Designer: Milo Anderson. I-2…Irene Dunne in *Penny Serenade* (1941). Designer: Uncredited. G-3…Greta Garbo in *Wild Orchids* (1929). Designer: Adrian. G-4…Greer Garson in *Random Harvest* (1942). Designer: Robert Kalloch. G-5…Greer Garson in *Mrs. Miniver* (1942). Designer: Robert Kalloch. J-6…Joan Crawford in *The Women* (1939). Designer: Adrian. B-7…Bette Davis in *All About Eve* (1950). Designer: Edith Head. B-8…Bette Davis in *Dark Victory* (1939). Designer: Orry-Kelly.

Evening Glamour… Whether the evening occasion was a ball, a cocktail party or languishing in the boudoir, every scene was costumed to make a fashion statement about the character and the star portraying her. G-1…Greta Garbo in *Inspiration* (1931). Designer: Adrian. J-2…Joan Crawford in *The Women* (1939). Designer: Adrian. I-3…Irene Dunne in *Love Affair* (1939). Designer: Howard Greer/Edward Stevenson. J-4…Joan Crawford in *The Bride Wore Red* (1937). Designer: Adrian. G-5…Greta Garbo in *The Painted Veil* (1934). Designer: Adrian. L-6…Loretta Young in *The Loretta Young Show* (1960). Designer: Travilla. G-7…Greer Garson in *Random Harvest* (1942). Designer: Robert Kalloch. I-8…Irene Dunne in *The White Cliffs of Dover* (1944). Designer: Irene.

Irene Dunne
Star of over 40 films including *Penny Serenade, Love Affair, I Remember Mama, Life with Father, A Guy Named Joe, Back Street, Magnificent Obsession, The Awful Truth, The Age of Innocence, Anna and the King of Siam.*

Greer Garson
Star of over 30 films including *Pride and Prejudice, Remember, Mrs. Miniver, Random Harvest, Blossoms in the Dust, Mrs. Parkington, Valley of Decision, Desire Me, Sunrise at Campobello, Julius Caesar* and *Goodbye, Mr. Chips.*

Greta Garbo
Star of over 30 films including *Flesh and the Devil, A Woman of Affairs, Anna Christie, Camille, Queen Christina, Ninotchka, The Painted Veil, Grand Hotel, Mata Hari, Romance, Anna Karenina, Conquest.*

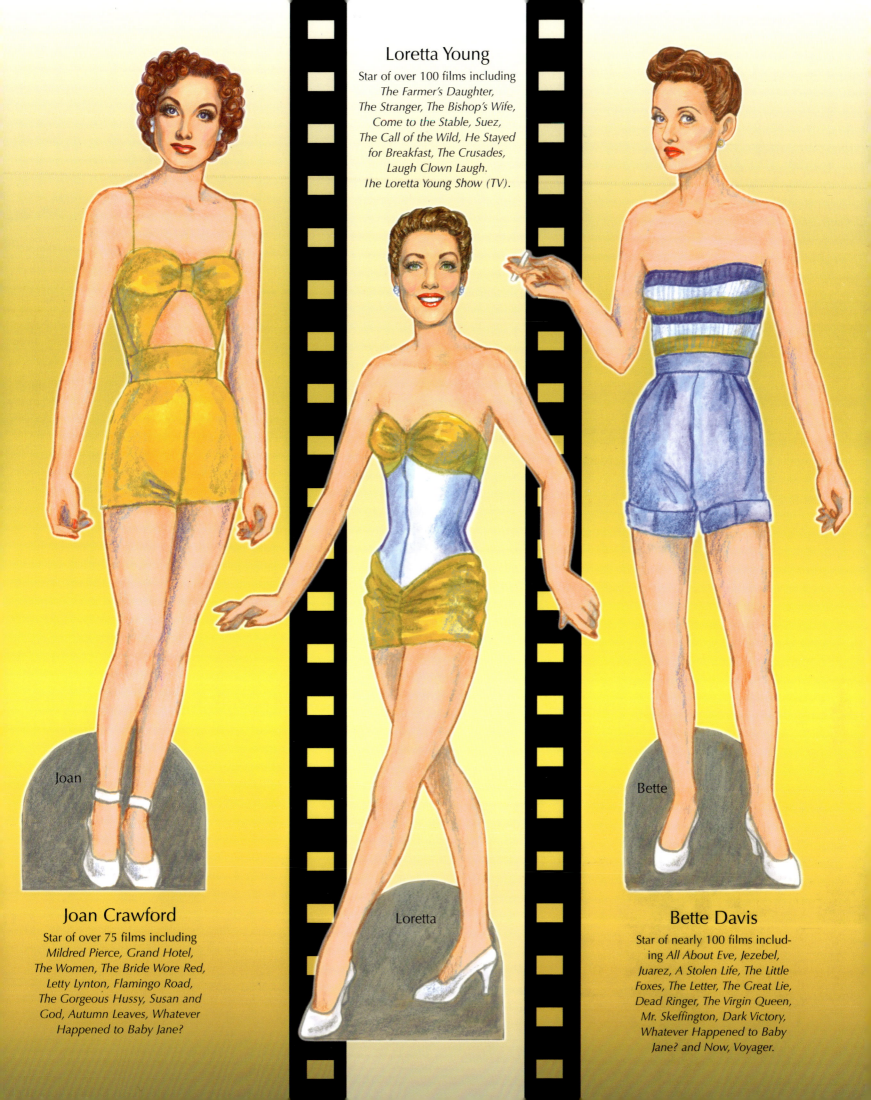

Character Roles… The star quality of a Drama Queen shone through costumed as a waitress, a Norwegian immigrant, a showgirl, a has-been child star or a stylish murderess. L-1…Loretta Young in *The Loretta Young Show* (1960). Wardrobe: Carey Cune. J-2…Joan Crawford in *Mildred Pierce* (1945). Designer: Milo Anderson. B-3…Bette Davis in *The Little Foxes* (1941). Designer: Orry-Kelly. I-4…Irene Dunne in *I Remember Mama* (1948). Designer: Edward Stevenson. G-5…Greer Garson in *Random Harvest* (1942). Designer: Robert Kalloch. B-6…Bette Davis in *Whatever Happened to Baby Jane?* (1962). Designer: Norma Koch. B-7…Bette Davis in *The Letter* (1940). Designer: Orry-Kelly. G-8…Greta Garbo in *Anna Christie* (1930). Designer: Adrian.

Leading Ladies... Star billing over the title when playing a Swedish Queen, a Parisian courtesan, a maid, an Empress of Mexico or a teacher in the royal court of Siam. G-1...Greta Garbo in *Queen Christina* (1933). Designer: Adrian. G-2...Greta Garbo in *Camille* (1936). Designer: Adrian. L-3...Loretta Young in *The Farmer's Daughter* (1947). Designers: Edith Head/Loretta Young. B-5...Bette Davis in *Juarez* (1939) Designers: Elmer Ellsworth/Ida Greenfield. I-9...Irene Dunne in *Anna and the King of Siam* (1946). Designer: Bonnie Cashin.

Period Pieces… Newsmaking costume trivia: This supposedly red gown in the black-and-white film was actually brown. Two of the 18 hoop-skirted gowns in *Suez* were replicas of Empress Eugenie's from the House of Worth. B-1…Bette Davis in *Jezebel* (1938). Designer: Orry-Kelly. L-2…Loretta Young in *Suez* (1938). Designer: Royer.